Ichabod

The Glory Has Departed
The Spiritual Poverty Of The Modern Church

Peter Kimathi

PUBLISHED by PARABLES
Earthly Stories with a Heavenly Meaning

Ichabod: The Glory Has Departed
The Spiritual Poverty Of The Modern Church
Peter Kimath

Published By Parables
August, 2019, 2019

All Rights Reserved. No part of this book may be reproduced or utilized in any form or by any means, electronic or mechanical, including photocopying, recording, or by any information storage and retrieval system, without permission in writing from the author.

    ISBN 978-1-951497-00-2
    Printed in the United States of America

Readers should be aware that Internet Web sites offered as citations and/or sources for further information may have been changed or disappeared between the time this was written and the time it is read.

ICHABOD
THE GLORY HAS DEPARTED
THE SPIRITUAL POVERTY OF THE MODERN CHURCH

PETER KIMATH

INDEX

One: The soil

Two: Lack of endeavor to launch dipper

Three: Moving before the " appointed" time

Four : Discover the will of God

Five: Nature of spiritual foundation

CHAPTER ONE

THE SOIL

As the rain and snow comes down from heaven, and do not return to it without watering the earth and making it bud and flourish, so that it yield seed for the sower and bread for the eater, so is my word that comes out of my mouth; it will not return to me empty, but will accomplish that I desire and achieve the purpose for which I sent it (Isaiah 55: 10 – 11).

In reference to the text, there is aspect that yearns ardent contemplation and dipper analysis. The rain fails not to water the ground but not all grounds are ideal for the plant to sprout. Anorther fact that should arouse your attention is that there is absolutely change once the rainfall pounds upon the ground. There is insight hidden in this passage that reveals the reason of failure and anchors the formulae of success.

Anybody who dreams of victory ought to fathom the text and implement it. "The rainfall fails not to water the ground." My word will not return to me empty." This refers to the effectiveness of the word of God that will definitely ignite results. The hindrance is," not all grounds are ideal for the plant to sprout".

The ground represents the contents of your heart. How you respond determines the results. The whole verdict lies on what you have harbored in your heart, your perceptions and what you open your heart to believe. The word will return empty if the ground (your heart) is hard and can't be penetrated. In your discretion, the farmer who ardently prepares his farm will receive the best share of the harvest. The preparation belongs to man; it is the duty of man to obliterate any false concepts, attitudes and belief that don't align with the word of God.

Prayers can't change your heart. This is dependence on your willingness to yield to the truth from the word of God. Mark that there is no lasting deliverance until you tame your thoughts. Many could be victors but have failed to tame their attitudes; consequently Satan has edge over their life. If Satan succeeds to entice you to believe a lie, and false concept, you to turn to be his captive. He has won over many potential victors who could be might men of valor but never was.

The wise man advices" guard your heart with all diligence for from it comes the issues of life (Proverbs 4:20)". Many don't take concern to the scripture, who turns prey to Satan wiles and craftiness. The term "guard" in the scripture should arouse your attention to stem absorbing teachings, concepts, that don't originate from the word of God. Beware what you open your heart to believe will shape and control your entire destiny. Many have receded to failures after failing to guard what they absorb.

The scripture mentions, "The issues of life". Absolutely you are what you believe, the issues of life will automatically surface and what is inside will be evidenced. How you respond, react and live will tell it all. There is no logic that can overthrow this fact; you are what you believe, what you have harbored in your heart is what dictates your life.

Despite much study on self-help concepts and philosophy, unless you get rid of garbage in your heart, you will achieve little.

Satan has changed tactics. He is aware that he can't overthrow the word of God, now he marshals his arsenal toward bombarding you with false concepts and beliefs.

Every form of teaching, belief, that has no scripture leaning originate from hell. These lies are carefully crafted to engross minds and divert people from the truth. These folks don't counter check teaching with the scriptures; believe falsehood who are on the highway to eternal doom unless retrieved early.

Any alteration to the immutable word of God will result to total failure. Prophet Joel reprimanded Israelites: render your heart and not your garments (Joel 2:13). It is apparent they strayed from God, indulged in falsehood yet feigned submission. Their hearts were far from God, something distinct had crept in and it was prevalent two seeds were growing in the same field.

THE GHOST MENTALITY

During the fourth watch of the night Jesus went out to them, walking on the lake. When the disciples saw him walking on the lake, they were terrified "it's a ghost", they said, and cried out in fear. But Jesus immediately said to them;" Take courage! It is I. Don't be afraid." (Mathew 14: 25-27).

The disciples attributed the supernatural occurrence to Satan works and little in regard to God might, they exclaimed " it is a ghost". This is terrible snare that has plagued many, who are delving to study much about satanic works, magic's and others of the sort. Once Satan succeeds to plant this snare in your heart, you will pose no threat to him. Scores are impressed to study much about Satan to their doom.

What lured them to be impressed by Satan works? Satan laid snare and they were trapped: victory was replaced with defeat; boldness with emaciation. These folks can't shake Satan nor even dare challenge him; he runs unchallenged and assume the victory stripped out in the Calvary.

There is absolutely no chance of triumphing in battle you are conscious your opponent has edge over you. He constantly convinces you how impregnable he is, all this is mere phantoms.

Ephesians 6:10 arouses us to put on full armor of God so that you can stand against satanic schemes. It is ultimately impossible to "stand" unless you are fully assured and firmly conscious in your spirit that: you have power to trample over all powers of the enemy (Luke 10:19).

This should not be just another confession; it should be deeply rooted in your spirit. He poses to be mighty when in reality he is subject to the saints in regard to the scripture.

The Pharisees claimed Jesus casted demons by Beelzebub" The prince of demons (Mathew 12:24). They crossed the boundary to study about Satan before acquainting with the might of God , consequently plugged into a snare. Belzebub was a false imagination that apparently bound their mentality.

The secret of David victory over Goliath was the virtue of being fully immersed into God might and the word of God claiming the prominent in his life. This is what he said; your servant has killed both lion and bear; this uncircumcised philistine will be like one of them, because he defied the army of living God (1 Samuel 17:36). There is nowhere he mentioned " giant" but this " uncircumcised philistine." He was too strong to be bound by " ghost mentality", a rare breed of Christians whom the word of God has taken preeminence. It is directly proportional; the more you know God, the more the "giants" recedes, the vice versa is detrimental.

THE HEART OF STONE

I will give you a new heart and put a new spirit in you; I will remove from you the heart of stone and give you a heart of flesh (Ezekiel 36:26).

There is no life in the stone; it can't be penetrated. The heart of stone refers to those who are obstinate to yield to the word of God.

Let explore what has hardened it.

1. Doubt

The book of Hebrews 3:12 says; see to it brothers and sisters that none of you has a sinful unbelieving heart that turns away from the living God. Unbelief usurps moral connection to God hence obliterate you completely from God presence. Those who choose doubt have sold their birthright to Satan. Faith is your birthright since; all is possible to him who believe(Mark 9:23). Esau despised his birthright who latter went ahead to miss his blessing (Genesis27:36) This is the terrible repercussion of doubt and how much you lose. Faith is our birthright and link of limitless provision from God.

Have you ever fathomed where doubt originated? Doubt originated in the garden of Aden, when Satan put "if" to the word of God. God had formerly warned Adam and Eve against eating the fruit at the middle tree but Satan said " if" you eat you shall be wise like God(Genesis3:5). The "if" makes God a liar. Doubt is not enigma, it is just inserting " if" to the word of God and you enroll into Satan register and sanctuary.

(3)Logic upon the word of God

Let me foremost expound that reasoning and logic are not vice, but turns detrimental when applied upon the word of God. There is no other vice that has hardened scores in this era than to reason upon the word of God rather than believe. This now turns Bible principles absurd and beyond reach.

What does the word to "believe" mean? According to dictionary explanation, to believe is to have trust. This trust is anchored by revelation and knowledge and God confirmation upon an individual. When you believe Him, then there is no place of reasoning upon His word since you are certain He will fulfill what he Has promised.

It is prominent in ordinary realm we walk by "assurance" based upon observation . Faith is anchored by total trust upon the word of God since His word can't fail. When you wait to be "assured" and be "certain" rather than trust the word of God, you have closed door to faith and wallowing at Satan domain. This is doubting the word of God.

The book of Proverbs 3:5 says: Trust the lord with all your heart and lean not on your own understanding. "Own understanding" is based upon logic hence dethroning faith and trust in God. Our understanding should be subject to the word of God because; no wisdom, no insight, no plan that can succeed against the Lord (Proverbs 21:30).

Note the term"all" in the scripture; trust the lord with all your heart. This deems simple, just another confession but implementing it is an uphill task. Can you trust the lord with all your heart like Abraham to sacrifice his only son, believing God will do a miracle of yet giving him another son despite being advanced in years? In reality we hardly trust the lord with all our heart but partially trust Him and at the same time divert to trust our logic and our own thinking.

ABSENCE OF SIGNS, WONDERS AND PROOF OF GOD PRESENCE

Doubt is emboldened by absence of veritable proof of God's presence. When there is absence of miracles, favour and answered prayers; the spirit of unbelief grips more firmly. This state was prevalent amongst Pharisee; the crowd was astonished and surprised by miracles performed by Jesus(Mathew 12:24). Their heart were hardened by unbelief, who were" surprised" since they didn't expect. When "surprises" and astonishment" replaces expectation, apparently doubt is abiding.

Most Christian gathering are regretfully miracle free-zones. They teach the Bible but it deem like another legend and once upon a time tale. Until what is learnt turns into reality, then you are reading a " dead" letter .When this state prevails the heart are hardened by unbelief and despondency creeps in.

Christianity devoid of signs and wonders is a sign of "wanting". Miracles affirms you are treading on right channel. Signs will follow those who believe(Mark 16:17). Once you choose to " believe" your life turn to be extra – ordinary. There is saying," miracles are not guarantee of entering heaven, but indicate you are on right track". I concur with this statement, it is good to be assured that I am on the course by God confirmation by signs, wonders and miracles.

Christianity is not an ordinary life unless we have deviated from sound doctrine. Jesus walked over the water as a sign He is above ordinary life (Mathew 14:25). The rest of the disciples except Peter were stuck at safe vantage at the bench (verse 29). Note that even the most rogue person can walk over the dry land(ordinary life), then what the distinction? If you are living a very ordinary life then there is something amiss.

Nicodemus was a teacher of the law, confidence in his duty but lacked stir. He was dry and almost natural who couldn't fathom what it mean to be born again (John 3:4) .If Nicodemus is your role model and your teacher, then you will likewise recede to be natural and ordinary.

THE HEART OF FLESH

And I will give you the heart of flesh(Ezekiel 36:26)

The heart of the flesh is permeable to the word of God. It is foremost worked over for the stormy nature to be peeled off. Despite the scripture saying," I will give you the heart of flesh," there is price inevitable. There is nothing automatic; logic proves it impossible for the storny nature to yield without being exerted force.

Let analyze the first step that the heart of stone pass.

Molding

The potter breaks the clay Mounds it into desired shape that is appeasing to the final consumer. The "mounding" process is not enjoyable, if the clay has voice, it could cry in great anguish in the hands of the potter.

God mounds us through trials, hardships to draw our attention to him. God took the giants of faith; Moses, Samson and David first in the bush to mound them before they come out in the public:Moses encountered God at the burning bush (Exodus 3:2-3), David killed lion and bear at the bush before confronting the ultimate challenge ;Goliath(1 Samuel 17:46).

Samson too had experience in the bush when he tore lion without much recognition (Judges 14:6). All had similar traits, they were prepared in the bush before they come out in the public. The bush experience is a mounding process that anchors assurance and confidence. They come out "knowing God" who had no place of presumption.

The wilderness experience is a mounding process alleged at breaking any other allegiance than God. It is also used to wean you from self-reliance to total dependence on God. He passed Israelites through wilderness to peel off Egyptian mentality, but the memory of "Lemons" and locubus" still lingered in their minds (Numbers 11:5). Those who imitate them are yet to surrender fully to the word of God, who have other solutions and remedies. Who are troublers in the church? Those who incite dissension strife and separations in the church? There those who come out half-baked, who turns Satan key target to exploit to his advantage. They had the calling, anointed but come out before the potter had finished with them. A trait prominent amongst them is that they are compromisers and yield to half-submission.

There is an example in the book of Acts 19:13-16: the sons of Sceva come out confidently but with limited knowledge, who turned easy prey to demons. These folks come from nowhere, and pressure to be somebody and demons granted them the price for their ignorance. They said,"In the name of Jesus, whom Paul preaches, I command you to come out " (verse 13) .Demons answered them, "Jesus we know, and about Paul we know , but who are you? " (verse 15). Apostle Paul came from somewhere, on the way to Damascus when he meet the Lord (Acts 9:3-5). He was molded, broken off his former rebellion and a new Paul was reborn. Did he come from nowhere?

2.   Rooted in Christ

Let read Colossians 2:7: "rooted and strengthened in faith as you are taught and overflowing with thanksgiving". There difference between "rooted" and "placed". The term "rooted" in the scripture emphasizes the magnitude of depth the word of God upon individual. To be "placed" is just vague belief that lapses in a moment.

A prominent character of those who possess the heart of flesh is they are rooted in the word of God and bears the fruits of active faith. As we analyze the journey of Israelites from Egypt to Canaan; the rest except Caleb and Joshua had no fruits of former miracles abiding in them (Numbers 14:2). The rest what they saw soon evaporated, consequently " giants" the might of God enshrouded, a sign of no fruits of former miracles abiding. They were example of "worthless fig (Mark 11:21).

Those rooted in Christ are immovable, stout and firm upon their confessions. Until you are rooted in faith, wavering and hesitations are inevitable. What holds us firmly is the conscious that God can't fail anchored by permeating your spirit with His word and always pondering His mighty works.

There is illustration about the two builders in Mathew 7:24-27, crucial to fathom. The parable distincts two builders; one built upon the rock and another built upon the sand. The one who build his building upon sand was washed away, the one built upon the rock was impregnable. When you believe the word of God and anticipate it, you are built upon the rock who is Jesus Christ. Who has never been defeated. Nothing can shake anybody who puts total trust in Him, no matter the intensity or magnitude .Those who puts trust in Him and not religion laughs at defeat.

WHY WE SHOULDN'T EXPECT QUICK RESULTS.

Then they brought him a demon posed man who was both blind and mute and Jesus healed him so that he could both talk and see. All the people were astonished and said " could this be the son of David?" But when the Pharisees heard this, they said, it is only by Beelzebub, the prince of demons that its fellow drives out demons (Mathew 12:22-24).

In regard to the text, it is apparent the healing of demon possessed man was much easy than breaking false belief bondage that had shackled them for years. They were utterly amazed, a sign of lack of expectation and unbelief abiding .Ultimately, false belief of "Beelzebub" was planted in their heart, which was firmly rooted and established to their doom.

Let me expound this fact vividly in reference to buildings. When erecting structures it is absolutely hard work that demands determination. Consequently, breaking it is a challenge, this now reflects breaking false belief that has lasted for centuries. Let me state it vividly that the belief is like fortified structure that breaking it is not easy, it demands patience and hard work. The immediate miracle was proof of legitimally of the scriptures, but the door was closed due to succumbing to believe error. If the Christians are slack to "" Go and preach the gospel to all nations " (Mark 16:15), Satan will go more hastily and preach a different message. Don't fool yourself, his message will be heard, the gospel of Beelzebub" will be implanted in peoples heart. The Pharisees alongside those who feign to be men's of God but alter with the scriptures are Satan servants.

This is what God instructed Jeremiah: Break and build, uproot and plant (Jeremiah 1:10). What God was referring is false worship, weird doctrines and vain worship. They should be " broken" and "uprooted" to plant and build sound doctrines. There are those who prefer to build upon weird structures (false doctrines) and plant good seed alongside bad seed, do dounting and vain work. There is no compromise here lest Satan hold on you. If you mix evil with good you will be wearing yourself with vanity toil and Satan will be the victor at the end.

It is recorded in Acts 14: 8-13; Apostle Paul raised the cripple ,the inhabitants unanimously concurred they were "gods" in human form. Despite apostle Paul and Silas reprove, they held upon their instinct and proceeded to sacrifice bulls to them even at their absence (verse 18). What should arouse your concern is the " false belief" that perpetuated in the city, and what a challenge to break it? Satan had gone before apostle Paul and won many converts except the invalid who opened his heart to believe the message preached and was healed (verse 9).

Nicodemus was fully convinced by the miracles performed by Jesus at the moment and rightly concurred: Nobody can do such things unless God is with him(John 3:2) .Nevertheless, the religious bondage was not lifted, he went to Jesus by night in fear of expulsion from synagogue. Nicodemus had at foremost work out his mind, obliterate false concepts and manmade inputs by aligning everything with the word of God. Despite Nicodemus having witness the miracles performed by Jesus, there is no miracle that can break mental despotic; renewing of the mind is the only paramount option.

The Gospel of Mathew 13: 1-8 narrates about a very critical topic that is the pillar of success. The parable illustrate about the sower who sowed good seed but latter the enemy sowed stalks at night, seizing the chance ceded by slumberness. Soon, it was prevalent two seeds were growing together consequently the whole harvest was ruined. Mark with great concern that God will only harvest " pure" seed; nothing " wanting" will find door to Him.

The parable brings into limelight how most are bound and shackled in false belief fetters. First, the enemy sows the seed; false beliefs and false teachings are sowed by Satan workers who feign as men's of God but instill falsehood contrary to the Bible.

Secondly, the recipient believes the lies and never aligns with the word of God to prove its legitimacy. What follow is the evil seed now sprouts which is vivid evidenced. The evil seed surfaces, creates character and shapes the entire destiny. These folks are now "bound," their character, confession and responses tell it all.

Peter Kimath

CHAPTER TWO

Lack of endeavour to launch " dipper",

Launch into the deep

When he had finished speaking, he said to Simon," put into deep waters, and let down the nets for a catch"(Luke 5:4).

In reference to the text, there those who know what ought to be done, but do it too shallowly. Jesus just reproved them ," Launch into the deep" he is saying to you," Launch into the deep in prayers, commitment and more earnest." There are those who are shallowly placed, frail who pose no threat to Satan. What prominent amongst them is they have no endeavor to press on to the ultimate price" (Philippians 3:14) they settle at stationary and confortable at yesterday manna, when there is portion for today (Exodus 16:21). There is " fish" in the deep; there is more revelation, greater impact if you endeavor to launch dipper!

The master is echoing the same statement now," launch into deep for a catch." He is willing you know Him in depths and greater magnitude. He knows that you are seeking Him but be more earnest. The door is wide open, only passivity and laxity poses as hindrance. Beloved, this is not the time to stroll nor be contented at meagle revelation about God, you have not yet seen what God has reserved to his saints (1 Corinthians 2:9). Are you ready to press on?

Our compatriot Abraham was fond of pitching tents in eve of moving forward (Genesis 13:18). Sadly, most due to limited knowledge have built mansions and settled at less the purpose of God when He is willing to give them more. The book of Lamentation 3:23 says: His mercies are new every morning. When you lose grip of yesterday visitation, miracles and triumph and press on for today's portion, then His mercies will be new every morning. His miracles, visitations will be likewise new every morning. Thank God and praise him for yesterday miracles and blessings but earnestly press for today's portion.

Jesus has no place for mediocrity;" Launch into the deep" arouses us to initiate big projects and carry out great exploits. The promise," whatever you wish ask" (John 15:7) is a wide open to ask great things and dream BIG. The door is wide open, only your perception can halt you. This is the right time to dream big, there is no humility in smallness.

When the disciples put the nets deep into the water in obedience to the master voice, they caught great houl of fish. This now refers to evangelism, are we putting more attention to the perishing world or are we just contented at religious obeisance's? Jesus expects us to be more earnest and passionate in seeking the lost at all means irrespective the cost. There are those who do it too shallowly, who have confined themselves and lulled at just reciting own initiated ways rather than " Launch dipper" to seek the lost. The master is not pleased with them since they hardly anticipate the great commission; preach the gospel to the whole creation(Mark 16:15).If we are in solidarity with this great commission, we are poised to hasten to seek the lost as the clock tickle's in bid to retrieve myriads who are on highway to perdition.

It is extremely irony how the same waters they caught nothing after Jesus intervention they caught great houl. Perhaps at the moment you are dormant, but there is great productivity in your bosom. How can you discover the vast endowment of your potential and talent unless you launch dipper? Hannah broke her bareness and birth one of the greatest prophet in Israel(I Samuel 1: 11-10) What spurred the miracle is the virtue she lost grip of passivity and dullness to seek God. There is greatness in your, if only you dare break passivity and endeavor to launch dipper into players, seeking God and more earnest in your spiritual walk.

Have you not fathomed that saints are powerful than Satan. Read Luke 10:19: "I have given you authority to trample on snakes and scorpions and to overcome all powers of the enemy; nothing will harm you". That plain truth; if you dare alter, you will cede great triumph to your adversary. However, this promise doesn't make us immune from Satan attacks. He preys on those who trend shallowly, until you flex spiritual muscle Satan will had edge over you.

Apostle Paul Silas prayed until prison parted asunder (Acts 16:20) .The prison had never before experienced such a force before; it had no option except to yield. If they could be frail and faint hearted like Christian of the time, who knows only the name of their denomination, the despotic could hold on the grip. The formulae to overcome is to " prove stronger", press on until the opposition yields.

" I will not let you until you bless me"

So Jacob was left alone and a man wrestled with him till day break. When the man saw that he could not overpower him, he touched the socket of Jacob hip so that his hip was wrenched as he wrenched wrestled with the man. Then the man said, let me go, for it is day break. " but Jacob replied," I will not let you go unless you bless me," The man asked him," what is your name?" "Jacob" he answered. Then the man said, " Your name will be no longer be Jacob, but Israel, because you have you have struggled with God and men and overcome(Genesis 32: 24-28).

The angel of the God told Jacob "Let me go for morning dawns." (verse26). Jacob was not earnest enough, he was not fervent. Nothing can hold God than earnestness and whole heartedly seeking Him. If you stroll, clamp and dullness prevails; you keep Him at bay. Passive spirit, casual prayers and slack in commitment can't hold God.

There are two things that deem related yet distinct; seeking God and holding him. Most seek God, and find him but fail to " hold on" that state. These folks are resolute in commitment but open loopholes hence God leaves them. Seeking God is coupled with cost and few hold him without bungling. Those who hold on God are those who; last works are better than the first(Revelation 2:9), those who detest conformity but hold on their confession to the end; those who start with spirit and with spirit, not with spirit and then flesh (Galatians).

God was amongst and His presence heavily felt among the early church. They were ardent, radical and stout in conviction. Acts 2:46 says; they continued steadfastly in prayers, breaking of bread and apostolic teachings.

They had more time for God and He had more time for with them; He confirmed his presence by miracles that perpetuated the whole environs.

They were extremely distinct with the current crop of Christians in this era whom strolling and slackness are prominent. They are almost "pushed" for everything; from service, offerings, and everything they must be pushed to respond. The call to great commission turns to be optional not priority. Jacob has an opportunity which he couldn't let it slip him. If you are presented with such opportunity, will you squander it? Jacob had a single chance which he seized to the utmost. His life drastically turned around and a new era dawned. But mark that there is aspect of alertness amiss in most who squander chances due to dullness most have let him "go" who are ever in dreary regrets.If you let slip any opportunity in your life, you let him "go", Beloved, let emulate Jacob, you may have just a single chance, don't let it "go"!

Note the term "until" in the scripture; I will not let you go until you bless me (verse 26) .There is no options; don't settle at anything less than real blessings and total victory. God will only grant request if you are wavering.

When you put "ifs" and "either" then you are not in full faith. Jacob said, I will not let you go until you bless me not "if you can bless me". Hold on until you receive "Isaac" not Ishmael (Genesis 17: 18-19. Most pray, hold on and when "Ishmael" surfaces they yield rather than press on until they receive "Isaac", total victory. Ishmael represents partial blessings and half- victory. The new name was pronounced after hefty, wrestling. If you are weared with the name "Jacob", the deciever, running away from Esau ,life full of defraundment, full of uncertainty, I counsel you to wrestle, time won't change anything.

There is wrestling with men, Satan and God: Jacob wrestled with all and prevailed (verse 29) .Wrestling with God is wonderful, it is challenging him to honour his word, coupled with prayers, thanksgiving and sacrificial offering. Most have wrestled with Satan and rob off what he has stolen from them, now wrestle with God to honor his word, until all promises are realty. If you dream of " New name", imitate Jacob not Hannah who waited until provoked to know the gate of the house of God (1 Samuel 1   ).

If God doesn't prevail over your life, Satan will. There is no middle ground; one of them has commanded the primacy. Godly ways has posed hefty and yearns extra- cost, most have deviated. Never resort to any other formulae if the word of God don't back it, better the hard way but sure. The other ways will pile trouble upon trouble, and finally damn you to eternal perdition. There are others blessed through other means than godly way don't envy them; although they are blessed, somebody is deprived basic wants for him to be where he is, somebody is widowed, orphanage for him to be driving that car. Always cling to godly ways, don't skip wrestling, spiritual warfare despite the cost rather than resort to dubious ways.

"See the son"

And there were shepherds living in the fields nearby, keeping watch over their flocks at night. An angel of the Lord appeared to them, and the glory of the Lord shone around them, and they were terrified. But the angel said to them," Do not be afraid, I bring to you good news of great joy that will be for all people. Today in this house of David a son has been born to you; you will find a baby wrapped in clock and lying in a manger. Suddenly host appeared with angels, praising and saying,

Glory to God in the highest, and on earth peace to all men on whom his favour rests.

When the angel had left them and gone into heaven, the shepherd said to one another," let's go to Bethlem and see this thing that has happened, which the Lord has told us about." So they hurried off and found Mary and Joseph, and the baby, who was lying in the manger. When they had seen him, they spread the word concerning what they had been told about this child, and all who heard it were amazed at what the shepherds said to them(Luke 2:8-18).

There are several lessons embedded in the passage very pertinent to grasp:

1. Rise above ordinary

There is peculiar aspect unveiled in regard to the shepherd attitude; they kept vigil at night when almost everybody was asleep. That's extra-ordinary indeed! They weathered night breeze at the expense of welfare of their flocks, an indication of rising above ordinary routine which should arouse our concern to ponder. They did extra- ordinary thing and saw extra ordinary occurrence .If anybody dreams to glimpse anything extra-ordinary, he is poised to emulate shepherd character.

Most Christians will be caught up in slumber at the advent of the Lord. The shepherds were live witness of His birth and those who hope to be caught up in the air at this second coming must unshackle from spiritual slumber. Many will be caught up in slumber and just as few witnessed his birth, the so called christians who are yet to yield to truth will be left behind. The shepherds saw what nobody else saw since the foundations of the world. Why did God choose this seemly obscure to glimpse this peculiar occurrence? There were teachers of the law, Pharisees, scribes whom at our opinion are the recipients of this rare visitation. However, there are conditions imperative if you dare grasp any supernatural visitation.

First, you must be spiritually alert. This is inner resolve to yield to the word of God and active in regards to godly thing, being alert in the spirit is obliterating every sin and indulgence in lawlessness.

Secondly, there is no revelation for passive Christians. The shepherd were active in their duty even at what deem to most of us as odd hours, we can only imitate them by abhorring slackness and stationary. The book of James 4: 8 says: come closer to God, and he will come closer to you. Wash hands you double minded. Make the first move and God will move towards you. Nobody will receive anything from God if he confines himself to stationary and passivity. The more you seek him, the more revelation, insights and wisdom you get. Don't expect anything if you don't make any move!

Thirdly we can't ignore associate factor. The shepherds had common goal, faith, confession and totally in unity.

Nobody had different opinion than " let us go and see the son" (verse) accompany the wise and you will be wise advices Proverbs 13:20. Don't expect any visitation, revelation and breakthrough if you associate with sects and contradicting doctrines. This is Satan lethal ploy that has derailed scores who have receded to be natural and ordinary. If you associate with doctrines that alter with the immutable word of God, mark that you are accompanying the enemies of God and you will be plagued with similar penalty.

2.   The light stage

" They saw the light" (verse 9)

They saw the light, which was just indication of what to come not the utmost. The " light stage" is just indication God is with you, not all that God has for you, the immediate blessings, favour and breakthrough are just " light stage", not all that He has for you. This nodes you to "press on" until you see the son; live to the fullest of God purpose towards you.

What if the shepherds " settled" at light stage and fail to pursue the message further? They could testify half-blessings and partial impact. Most have stuck here, they boast of meager blessings when God could grant them more if only they endeavor to press on.

Abraham was fond of pitching tent in the eve of moving on to the next phase of blessings (Genesis 13:18). He was convinced God has more blessings for him, hence he didn't build permanent residence since God will move to an another level. If we really emulate Abraham and outright heirs of faith, we ought not build masons on immediate miracles and blessings, since there are more! Be nomads, just pitch tent, you are moving on!

What I am convincing you is you should not "settle" where you are currently, that just the " light stage". There are more that God has for you, if you unshackle yourself from fake contentment.

Apostle Paul makes me crazy. This is what he said," I am pressing towards the ultimate prize (Philippians 3:14). Somebody who performed extra-ordinary miracles (see Acts 19:11) is still endeavoring to "press on". Do we have Christians who emulate him? How can you imitate him when you are confortable at miracle free zone, life that don't portray any trait of God presence? Apostle Paul is one of the rare breed of Christians who are insatiable for God and He has more room for them. If you seek me with all your heart you will find me (Jeremiah 29:13) .If you " Settle" at one level, you are not seeking God, we seek him when we are hungry for more revelation, wisdom and more concerning God.

Ichabod: The Glory Has Departed

There is a journey

The shepherds said to one another; " let us go and see what the Angel has told us" (verse10). There is absolutely price to pay, if you dream to turn the word into reality. The Bible says: strive to enter by the narrow door(Mathew7:13) as soon as Zion travailed she birth her sons (Isaiah 66:8). This point to us that there is price and cost inventiable. Teaching that deny this fact is false and has no scripture learning.

The journey entails exploring why the word is not real in your life. Seek out rather than be confortable at miracle free zone. Ask yourself, do I fulfill all moral obligations? Is there hidden sins I have not exposed and repented. Unless you answer yourself these questions, you will live to confess the word but never reality in you.

Take concern that what written in the Bible is not beyond grasp. Whatever written can be utmost real and evidenced if only you endeavor to pursue it further. The ultimate reason the word turns unrealistic is mixing divine with logic. Due to obsession with ordinary occurrence and remedies, the word recedes to be another history and tale. The church turns to be a gathering place, a club or just another place of meeting.

There those who rather than pursue the word, change denomination to another. This is vain wandering that most have resorted, despite their wandering they are left empty since nothing will unfold until the recipients open the door of their heart.

This is the order; read the word, believe it, then implement it. When you implement it, then it turns into reality. This now anchors assurance and emboldens confidence. Scores who are wallowing in delusions and dubious doctrines skip these simple and proven formulae who eventually turn prey to man's craftiness and wiles.

Jesus proclaimed in Luke 4:21; "This day the scripture is fulfilled in your hearing". The crowd were filled with astonishment since they didn't expect the one prophesied to appear in human form at that time. Due to long duration, it deemed to them like a fancy imagination and phatoms, but it was fulfilled as the scripture prophesied (see Isaiah 42:7). This is the challenge: are you reading the scriptures" expecting" it to be reality or you are just reciting it day after day? "This day the scripture is fulfilled at your hearing". Beloved, graduate from just reading the word to its fulfillment. The scripture is fulfilled today in you; his blessings, healing and every promise fulfilled in you. The master is echoing the same to you as He said to them. Never settle at anything less, overcome every hurdle, pay every cost and press on until" all that is written is fulfilled in you".

Absolutely if the word is real in you and experiencing and anticipating the promises of God, it is hard to be duped. If you firmly "know" and not presuming, then you have overcome the trap of deception.

Fake contentment

The shepherds could be contented at first stage; the light stage, but this is "fake" contentment. There are those who are confortable at miracle free-zone, mediocrity and life that doesn't portray the image of God. Most could be contented at light stage, but this rare breed of Christianity never settle at less than; seeing the son, the word being reality and anticipating God promises.

There exists good contentment and fake contentment. The distinction is prevalent: Good contentment gives glory to God for immediate miracles, but yet endeavor to press on to the ultimate; they open their mouths wide to be filled(Psalms 81:10). Fake contentment has no endeavor to press on and has no testimony.

The following are the characteristics of healthy contentment

> 1. Give thanks for immediate miracles, blessings and breakthrough, but yet press on because; you have not seen what God has reserved for his saints(1 Corinthians 2:9).

2. Take immediate miracles, blessings and breakthroughs as stepping ground to higher level. Today's miracles and blessings are proof God is with you, not the utmost. There is more and more that God is willing to grant you if only you don't "settle" at immediate miracles.

They were witness:

The shepherds were witness of what they saw; when they had seen him, they spread the word concerning what had been told about this child (Verse 17), Today there are few witness, what can you witness unless you have experienced it? I witness blessings because I am blessed, I witness deliverance, because am delivered, I witness goodness of God, because I have tasted it. There are those who speak what they heard about, but real witness speak of what they know and touched; that what was from beginning, which have seen with our eyes, which we have looked at and our hands have touched this we proclaim concerning the word of life (1 John 1:11). God want you to see the son; see your blessings, breakthroughs and experience what God has promised. The angel told the shepherds," you will see the son wrapped in cloth and lying in a manger " (verse 12). your blessings " there," go and get it!

If only you believe the word of God and pursue it, you will see the son(blessings, miracles and every promise of God will be real. The shepherds saw the son as the Angel told them: everything written is poised to be grasped, It's there; it's not once upon a time myth.

Don't yield to have a second hand experience; have personal experience. Have own testimony, speak what you have witnessed not necessarily what you have heard about. The door is wide open- " go and see the son" Follow the word and it will be real in you, why succumb to be a second hand experience?

There is nobody closer to God than others, the price is the same and door opened to everybody. This is faulty belief that has engulfed many who erroneously allege there are individuals " more" closer to God than others. This faulty belief breeds " dependency" when everybody is welcomed to the throne of grace; let us approach the throne of grace with confidence, so that we may find mercy and find grace to help us in time of need (Hebrews 4:16).

If you can't see him " now" you won't see him at His second coming

How can you expect to see Jesus at his second coming when you don't see him now. The shepherds had a special privilege to glimpse him at birth, but when he will return; every eye will see him (Revelation 1: 7). Don't fool yourself, what hindering you from experiencing His might now will hinder from being caught up in the air at his advent.

This is the gauge, unless you are experiencing His might now, walking by his presence and fully immersed into Him, do your homework before you are doomed at the last hour. Time is too short for self- deception, if you can't walk over water like him, there is carnal aspect you possess (see Mathew 14:28).

Even the most rogue person can walk over dry land then what is the distinction? Walking over water refers to experiencing God presence, miracles and raising above "ordinary" plane of life.

CHAPTER THREE

Discover the will of God

This is the confidence we have towards approaching God: that if we ask anything according to his will, he will hear us(1 John 5:14).

The term " according to his will" in the scripture should raise your attention to contemplate it in depth . Most ignore it, and never endeavor to explore it significant who plunge into defeat. Don't just yourself, if you pray not "according to his will" you will be opening a closed door which is drudgery and daunting. Despite how long you spend, all will culminate to vanity toil.

Before moving further, let draw example from Jesus prayer in Luke 22:42: Fathers if you are willing take this cup from me; yet not my will, but yours be done. The cup was horrible indeed, but it was the will of God that He suffer for human redemption. Do we imitate Jesus to put these words after presenting our requests; "yet not my will, but your will be done. The will of God is irrevocable, we can't triumph contrary despite how long you pray nor any sacrifice.

Apparently, unless you align with the will of God, defeat is imminent. There is will of God concerning your life: Prayer can't change it, have you ever contemplate the consequences that could unfold if God granted Jesus request; First we could be destined to hell since his imminent death and resurrection atoned our sins and opened way to Gentiles to enter the kingdom of God. Secondly, Satan could grip over humanity forever, since his defeat at Calvary landed us full victory. Thirdly, Satan could still be holding the keys of death at hades, which Satan took when he died and resurrected (Revelation 1: 18).

The will of God possess the following characteristics

1. Does not contradict with the scriptures

The will of God does not contradict with the scriptures everything godly must align with the word of God, I mention must because there is no other door, unless you enter by the window hence a robber and thief (John 10:8). Any slight deviation is categorically outside the will of God; this is the gauge, shun anything outside the scriptures.

Scores have been damned and duped by false prophets and false teachers whom even their character don't conform to the scriptures. They come with charming messages claiming; " I bring the will of God" but are mastermind of apostasy. Many have turned prey to such wiles after failing to hold fast the scriptures as the ultimate guide book. Beware to follow people dogmatically unless they pass the text of legitimacy. What spurred the young prophet doom in 1 kings 13: 18-24, is heeding to man rather than hold on God instructions. The old prophet deluded the young prophet and that marked the abrupt demise of his promising ministry. If you sense any alteration of the scriptures, that apostasy, run away hastily.

The young prophet is not alone, the list is much larger. Those who follow cultic and sects are his cohorts who will fall into similar ditch unless retrieved early? There was a leaper who told Jesus," If you are willing, make me clean". (Mathew 8:2). Jesus replied, "I am willing, be clean" (verse 3). In this case, you don't have squander much time the word of God affirms, " it is the will of God to be healed". Jesus come to destroy the works of the devil; sickness, curses and all predicament are works of the devil. Jesus come to destroy all!

2. The will of God does not bring regrets

The will of God is accompanied with great peace, satisfaction and ever live to testify God's goodness and faithfulness. There are those who are ever engulfed in remorse and in bitter regrets. We can certainly concur they treaded outside the will of God.

Nobody who ever followed the will of God in the whole Bible ever come to regret. They were full of joy, who are fundamentists of our faith. Their move was marked by God and what they embarked was confirmed mighty signs, wonders and outright proof of God presence. " I wish I know" is found amongst those who disdain God will and opt to obey their carnal " desires". They yielded to their emotions rather than the word of God and now they are in bitter remorse. The Holy spirit reprieved them consistently but the other voice of the enemy prevailed to their doom.

3.   The will of God aligns to the purpose of God concerning your life

The will of God will always be in harmony with the purpose of God concerning your life. Read Genesis 16: 1-2

Now Sarah had borne him no children. But she had an Egyptian maidservant named Hagar; so she said to Abraham," The Lord has kept me from having children,

Go sleep with the maid servant perhaps, I can build a family through her."

Verse 15:

So Hagar bore Abram a son, and Abram give him the name Ishmael to the son she had borne.

Abraham yielded to his wife and bore Ishmael contraly to Gods will that a son will born by Sarah shall be the apparent heir. Isaac was the will of God; Ishmael was the plan of man and his own desires, if you yield to anything contrary to the purpose of God, that is Ishmael.

Ishmael refers to the following:

1. Ishmael refers to "flesh" desires. Those lend by carnal desires end up birthing Ishmael. This is the apostasy and contradictions prevalently evidenced. When the flesh desires fully grow, give birth to "Ishmael", who now stands in place of" Isaac".

The carnality overthrows the divine and what implants itself is indulging in human remedies, usurping divine principles and ordinances.

2. Ishmael is settling less than God purpose for your life. Are you living to the utmost of your potential and purpose? Have you yielded to less? David was

endowed with potential to kill Goliath not just " bear" and " lion" (1 Samuel 17:34). If you settle at " bear" and "lion" level when you are endowed with potential to kill Goliath then you have birthed " Ishmael", The will of God is you exploit your talent and potential to the utmost and unturn every stone.

3. Ishmael is fake contentment and lack of endeavor to press on (Philippians 3:14). These folks feast on Yesterday manna and never collect today's portion , There is manna for today (yesterday visitation and miracles are good but there is still portion for today).

Press on, don't stroll, there is much to possess and fulfill. Turn every stone, fulfill your mandate and make sure you give servant food at right – time (Mathew 24:45). God demands promptness, if you stroll, mark you are out of His way!

4. Ishmael is associating and linking with weird worship and bad spiritual foundation. Myriads in this era have plunged into cultic and dubious doctrines that have no learning to godliness. A prominent trait is absence of veritable proof of God presence. It is the will of God that you link to " live" churches that bears fruits of active faith as portrayed in the book of Acts of apostles and victory preeminence.

5. Ishmael is partial obedience;yielding to half obedience is total disobedience.

The will of God is you obey all His laws (Joshua 1:6).Trust the Lord with all your heart (Proverbs 3:5).Partial obedience has usurped the church the glory and drained the anointing. This cedes Satan easy spot to moul you, never deceive yourself unless you obey all laws of God, forget divine intervention. The current church lack stir and little of divine manifestations due to succumbing to half submissions and "half's" in almost everything.

6.   Ishmael is exulting men, religion and own initiated systems above God .Who are you making known; God or his servant? This is the terrible snare that most have plunged. It is alarming since most denominations knew the servant of God than God himself. This vice is old like Bible itself; when you read the book of Exodus 32:1-5: it accounts that after Moses strayed in the Mountain, immediately people lost faith in God.

7.   Ishmael is fighting the "anointed of God; this is declaring war against God even when many folks disquise it as upholding the divine way. This is crossing the boundary, hence categorically Satan Pointmens.The Pharisees fought Jesus all the way feigning to be legitimate but were Satan's pointmens. Their dynasty was devoid of stir and clawless.

Regretly, this vice is rampant in most churches who claim to guard against the truth but fight the same truth.

How to discern the will of God

1. The word of God

The word of God is ultimate will of God. There is nothing that can supersede it; it the ultimate guidebook and whatever it says is the will of God. The will of God conforms to the word of God. Before anticipating anything, ask yourself," Does the word of God back it"? if not, then shun it completely.

2. Inner voice

There are instances despite the word of God backing it, yet the Holy spirit guide otherwise, there is incident recorded in acts 16:6, Paul and his companions were restrained by Holy spirit to spread the regions of province of Asia, in this obscure incident, preaching is not wrong but it is shrewd to obey the Holy spirit guidance, defiance is outright rebellion and this will stifle intimacy with God. Discernment is paramount in such incidences and this vary upon individual capability to discern. There is no revealed procedure but individual discernment is what paramount. Everybody filled with Holy spirit is in position to discern accurately. Jesus said, " My sheep hear my voice" (John 10:3) .Everybody who belongs to him is in position to hear his voice perfectly.

3. The peace of God

The peace of God that surpasses all understanding will accompany those who tread upon the will of God (Philippians 4:7) .Ultimately, the peace of God will confirm to you that you are walking on right path. If there exist condemnation in your spirit, then that a sign that there is something wrong. The peace of God will be accompanied by the following;

1. There will be no condemnation and guilt

(2) You will tend to be comfortable and enjoy what you are doing

(3) Joy and gladness will replace sorrow and condemnation

(4) Your conscious will be calm and always feel at ease.

Prayers can't change the will of God

When you ask, you don't receive, because you ask with wrong motives that you may spend what you get on your pleasures (James 4:3).

Mark that prayers prevails when there is no alteration with the will of God. The scripture categorically affirms; we ask and we don't receive", not all asking is granted.Jesus request to have the cup removed was not granted. God knows your motive even before you ask and will only grant what streamline your intimacy and His purpose in you.

God will not grant prayers on the following grounds:

> 1. When you ask for selfish ambitions and interests. What the purpose of your prayer? Will it glorify God and streamline your relationship and intimacy with him? Unless your prayers conform to this fact, don't expect any response.

Simon asked the apostles power for selfish interest: "Give me this ability so that everyone on whom I lay my hands may receive the Holy Spirit "(Acts 8:9). There are many in this era with motive similar to Simon, despite spending much time in prayers closet, yet God turns deaf to their requests. Since He knows their motives, you will discover that those with motives similar to Simon endeavor to build their own names, reputations, own agendas and not the kingdom of God. God granted Hannah request for a son because it complied with the purpose of the kingdom, she didn't ask to avenge to his co-wife provocation and that pleased God (1 Samuel 1:11). Will the breakthrough, favour, promotion you are asking take you closer to God? If it will cause you to stumble, then better to pluck that eye than go to hell with two eyes (Mathew 5:29) .

2) Prayers are act of presenting "requests" not complains. Philippians 4:6 says: "let your requests be known to God. Hannah formerly presented complains until Eli presented request :"Don't take for your servant for a wicked woman; I have been praying here out of my anguish grieve"(1 Samuel 1:10) .Praying in " anguish and "grieve" is presenting complains not requests. God demands you approach Him in fervertness and gentleness. later Eli replied," go in peace, and my the God of Israel grant you want you have ask of him " (verse 17). Eli presented request and it was granted.

3) Prayers are answered at right time, God will grant your request at appointed time, don't allege that He hasn't heard you.

Daniel interceded for release of Jews from captivity in Babylon (Daniel 9:1-17) since the seventy years prophesied by prophet Jeremiah was over but the captivity was lifted and they were released in the time of king Cyrus (Ezra 1: 1-4).

4. God will answer prayers that don't alter with his intended purpose for each individual. Let read Mathew 20:20-23:

Then the mother of Zebedee sons came to Jesus with her sons kneeling down and asking something from him. And he said to her," what do you wish? She said to him," grant that those sons of mine may sit, one on your right hand and the other on the left, in your kingdom". But Jesus answered and said, " you do not know what you ask. Are you able to drink; and be baptized with the baptism that I am baptized with? " They said," we are able". So he said to them," you will indeed drink my cup, and be baptized with baptism that I am baptized with; but to sit on my right hand and on the left is not mine to give, but it is for those whom it is prepared by my father.

There is intended purpose for each individual that why Jesus didn't grant the sons of Zebedee request. God will never accept any prayer that don't conform with His purpose for each individual. Jesus replied to their request that " to sit on my right and on my left hand is not mine to give, but it is for those whom it is prepared by my father". There is what God has prepared for you, your gifts and ministry, just pray that He unveil it not what you wish.

CHAPTER FOUR

Moving before the "Appointed Time"

Once more the Philistine raided the valley; so David inquired of God again, and God answered him," Do not go straight up, but circle round them and attack them in front of the balsam trees – as soon as you hear of the marching in the tops balsam trees, move out to battle, because that will mean God has gone out in front of you to strike the philistine". So David did as God commanded him, and they struck down the philistines army, all the way from Gibeon to Gezer (1Chronicles 14:13-16).

There is obscure aspect revealed in text paramount to fathom, ultimately the pillar of success. Why did God request he wait until he hears the matching on top of balsam tree? What could be the consequences of moving before? In answer to these questions shed great insight on why we should move on appointed time; not before nor after.

David could fail when he was poised to victory. There is no logic that can overthrow this fact; if you dare disdain it, you will plunge into utter defeat. Another peculiar aspect to ponder is how did David heard the "marching on top of balsam trees". This is wholly dependence on individual discernment.

As we refer to the story of Joseph in Genesis 31; what apparent is he spoke words out of season. The dream was correct but spoke to wrong people in wrong time. His brethren's out of indignation unimously plotter his demise. If not for God mercy, his dream could have ended in grave. You have fantastic dream alright, but wait upon ideal time and right people to unveil it.

There is no positive aspect to emulate from Joseph, if you dare imitate him, your dreams will vanish like smoke. Although God was sympathetic towards Joseph for his inadequate wisdom, I don't hope he will towards you. There is likelihood of abortion of destiny unless you guard your tongue and discern to whom you open your inner chamber and at what time.

The book of 1 kings 13: Narrates of a folk whom this topic was enigma to him. The young prophet doom was spurred by inadequate wisdom. He was mighty in power but "wanting" in terms of wisdom who aborted his promising destiny. Probably if he could opt to conceal that God had told him not to eat anything, he could have overcome the trap. He divulged the secret too early to his doom, ceding chance Satan to maul him.

If you read almost all gospel, there instances that Jesus warned against exposing the miracles to the public.

He accompanied three out of twelve disciples to the mountain of transfiguration because what was evidenced was not supposed to be exposed at that time. Do we really follow Jesus footsteps? If we are in allegiance with him, then we should choose what to expose and conceal and at what time.

How to discern the right time

In reference to the scriptures, there are three key means to identify and discern the appointed time:

1. Being fully equipped

I am going to send to you what my father has promised; but stay in the city until you have been clothed with power from high (Luke 24:49).

Have you ever contemplated the reason why Jesus commended them to stay in the city until endowed with power from high? Foremost, Jesus knew the intensity of the task ahead, the opposition they will face and the enemy who is lurking to maul them; who dares weak opponent. Secondly he was conscious of the task ahead that is only possible through divine empowerment.

Jesus predicted to Peter that he will deny him which he denied: "immediately the cock crowed the second time. Then Peter remembered the word Jesus had spoken to him; " "Before the cock crows twice you will down me three times. And he broke down and wept" (Mark 14:72). Formerly he said; "Even if I have to die with you, I will never disown you," and all others said the same (verse 31). What Jesus was pointing is Peter weakness which he was adamant to concede. At this stage, he was "wanting" and not fully equipped. God never rejects us on account of weakness but is patient that we mature in character . He is in process of molding us to be vessel of honor if only we yield to his reproval. .

The bold Peter the Pentecost is distinctly different from the one who disowned Jesus (see Acts 2:-40). Peter who denied Jesus was called and destined to greatness but was not fully equipped for the task. What a terrible blunder for the Peter who disowned Jesus to assume full responsibility and service?

The terrible consequence is he could dent and sabotage what he could accomplish.

God don't reject us due to our shortcoming and lapses in character, but He is patient with us until we mature in grace and character. If only we are patient enough to pass the molding process we will come out beaming.

This is what prophet Samuel told Saul." When you see those sign, then move on, because God is with you" (1 Samuel 10:17). A key word to contemplate is " when these signs appears then move". This depicts full assurance God is with you and fully equipped for the task. Signs will appear as a confirmation God is with you and He has approved you for the task ahead. Then move out and embark on your task confidently.

God prepared his servants of old in style: Moses met God at the burning bush (Exodus 3:1-9), when he experienced the might of God before confronting Pharaoh. David was prepared in the bush before confronting the ultimate challenge:Goliath (1samuel 17). David and Joseph, the two giants of faith had similar positive trail to emulate; they acted promptly buoyed by their inner conviction.

Easter could end just an ordinary woman until an opportunity for a new queen unfolded. Vashti fell out of favour. The king declared the post of queen vacant (Easter 2:17). She prepared herself for six months and headed to his uncle advice conceal his identity and this heralded her to triumph, she went ahead to the ultimate Saviour of the Jewish community in the kingdom. The chance arose appropriate time when Satan had devised ploy to quash all Jews in the empire.

2.   Divine guidance

Divine guidance is enigma to most, but it in existence and one way of discerning the appropriate time. There are several incidents recorded in the Bible that God directed various individuals through dreams, visions, and prophesy. When you read 1 kings 17:7-8) after the brook dried up. God directed Elijah to widow at Zeraphath who was prepared for that particular moment.

Religious folks deny that their exist divine guidance yet anchored in the scriptures. Nothing has changed with time, modern technologies and trends can't render divine ways ineffective.

It is paramount to note that divine guidance is devoid of error. As we cite the incident of Elijah, everything worked as God directed him. If only you are sure of God guidance be certain there is no place of faltering.

CHAPTER FIVE

Nature of spiritual foundations

What is foundation?

According to dictionary explanation, foundation is the most basic part of something from which the rest of it develops. The other explanation is "the part of the building that is below the ground and that supports the rest of the building. These two explanations vividly depict that foundation is the basic part that the rest develops hence everything natural and spiritual develops from something; its foundation.

When foundation is concerned, there is spiritual foundation just as there exist natural foundation. Spiritual foundation refers to where you have based your belief- what you believe and pay allegiance. There are diverse beliefs in the word and each "belief" now forms the spiritual foundation.

Scores in this era due to being shallowly placed and inadequate knowledge have plugged into weird spiritual foundation. This has marked the onset of their doom, despite feigning to be in pursuit of truth. These folks joined congregation due to many other factors and failed to observe the most paramount factor; the nature of spiritual foundation.

This topic is what dictates success and the reason of failure is bound to it as far as spirituality is concerned. Never assume to walk in power of God's until you stand upon good spiritual foundation.

Let read 1 Corinthians 3:10-11; By the grace God has given me, I laid a foundation as an expert builder, and someone else is building on it. But each one should be careful how he builds. For no-one can lay foundation other than the one already laid, which is Jesus Christ. We learn the following from the text;

1. Apostle Paul build the foundation of the new testament by grace of God. He was instructed by Holy Spirit not by own intuition. He was chosen vessel to build New Testament foundation and God confirmed by powerful sign, wonders that followed.

2. Those who build upon other foundations than this build by Apostle Paul are sects, cults and contradicting doctrines that have deviated from the truth. Apostle Paul put it clear; I build, the others built upon it". The foundation is already laid, there is no other; any other is alteration which will lead to great error.

(3) There is no slight distortion; you are either outright correct or wrong. There is no pace of being "closer" to this truth. This is lethal trap which many have plunged who you are on highway to perdition. God demands; obey all his commandments (Mathew 28:20). There is no place of being "closer" or "almost", kill all the "baals" (1 kings 18).

4. The foundation is clear: the word of God, adherence to it, you are dead sure of pursuing the right path. It is absurd and detrimental to follow doctrines without scriptures backing, at the end it will prove daunting and will be characterized with defeat.

Keys to discern the nature of spiritual foundation

Discerning of weird spiritual foundation prompts alertness and acquaintance with the scriptures. This is not a matter of physical observation, it yearns inner discernment. This is only possible by help of Holy Spirit and aligning everything with the word of God. Most have turned victims of such weird foundations, who have been allured and charmed by other factors.

There is no other consideration that can surpass the nature of spiritual foundation. This is the fatal bladder most make who are wallowing in doctrines whom God don't approve.

However, this is extremely enigma to shallowly based Christians. Discernment is for nature Christians who have permeated their spirit with the word of God. This now prompts you to graduate from just listening to studying the word of God in depth. Sects and cultic movement has taken root and spread like wild fire due to most are obsessed to miracles and lack of endeavor to counter check everything with the word of God.

The following are keys to discern and identity the nature of spiritual foundation follows:

1. Founders

The founder of any church has a link and influence spiritually to his associates. What was his motive, prospects and vision? If his vision was evil, consequently his followers are standing upon weird spiritual foundation, Amos 3:3 asks:" can two walk together unless they agree."

Absolutely, joining any church is linking with the covenant and there is outright link into the spiritual world. This fact carries great significant yet most disdain it.

There is another pertinent question to ask yourself," did he dedicate the organization to the wicked spiritual realm and partaken evil covenant"? If he dedicated it to God, then there will be confirmation by signs, wonders and outright proof of God presence.

2. Worship

What do they worship? Do they wholly follow the word of God? Is there any other ritual, allegiance they instill that is not Bible oriented? The answer to these questions is key to discover and analyze the credence of the spiritual foundation. What you exult above God is what you worship.

There those who feign to worship God but in truth they are worshipping their tradition, formulas, systems and other things. This is because they hold fast their own systems than the word of God.

3. Oaths

There are oaths that don't align with the word of God, any oath, swearing that don't align with the word of God opens door to demonic influence. Those who partake these oaths despite feigning to follow the scriptures are definitely standing upon weird spiritual foundation.

4. Teaching

Do they teach the whole Bible or they alter and teach part of it? If there exist any alteration that is weird spiritual foundation. Where there exist alteration with scriptures wittingly, you don't need anybody to tell you, the Bible probes them weird.

Heresies has bloomed in these last days and many who regard sound doctrine as burdensome and outdated has boarded bus to eternal perdition. The narrow door has posed too demanding, the wide door has found many entrants.

There is another form of apostasy amongst those who presume to be impeccable. They don't believe in the fivefold ministry. They believe some gifts and shut door to other gifts. This is apostasy and out of order. The word of God is the only ultimate guide, nobody can improve it. Either you are correct or utmost wrong.

Ichabod: The Glory Has Departed

Peter Kimath

Ichabod: The Glory Has Departed

Ichabod: The Glory Has Departed

Peter Kimath

Ichabod: The Glory Has Departed

www.ingramcontent.com/pod-product-compliance
Lightning Source LLC
Chambersburg PA
CBHW050204130526
44591CB00034B/2101